MADONNA

by
Jill C. Wheeler

Visit us at
www.abdopub.com

Published by ABDO & Daughters, an imprint of ABDO
Publishing Company, 4940 Viking Drive, Edina, MN 55435.
Copyright ©2003 by Abdo Consulting Group, Inc.
International copyrights reserved in all countries. No part of
this book may be reproduced in any form without written
permission from the publisher.

Printed in the United States.

Graphic Design: John Hamilton
Cover Design: Mighty Media
Cover photo: Corbis
Interior photos:
    AP/Wide World, p. 1, 7, 8-9, 12, 19, 21, 27, 29, 33, 34, 37,
        39, 43, 47, 49, 51, 57, 62
    Corbis, p. 5, 11, 15, 16, 23, 24, 30, 40, 45, 53, 55, 58, 59,
        60-61

Library of Congress Cataloging-in-Publication Data

Wheeler, Jill C., 1964-
    Madonna / Jill C. Wheeler.
        p. cm. — (Star tracks)
    Includes index.
    Summary: Describes the life and career of the popular
American singer, actress, and businesswoman.
    ISBN 1-57765-768-3
        1. Madonna, 1958—Juvenile literature. 2. Singers—
United States—Biography—Juvenile literature. 3. Motion
picture actors and actresses—United States—Biography—
Juvenile literature. [1. Madonna, 1958- 2. Singers.
3. Women—Biography. 4. Rock music.] I. Title. II. Series

ML3930.M26 W54 2002
782.42166'092—dc21
[B]
                                    2001058951

CONTENTS

MADONNA
MANIA

IN THE SUMMER OF 2001, MADONNA launched her first tour in more than eight years. After nearly 20 years in the spotlight, Madonna's fans still couldn't get enough of her music and dancing.

Madonna has become more than an entertainer. She's a cultural icon. Several universities, including Harvard, have offered classes about Madonna and how she has influenced American culture. Scholars still try to figure out how one person can strike so many chords with the public.

Madonna has always craved attention. She made herself into a star. "I'm normal height," said the five foot four-and-a-half inch performer. "I have a normal figure. I don't sing any better than other people. In fact, there isn't anything on the outside of me that is in any way abnormal. I think it's what's underneath, on the inside, that is not normal."

Since she burst onto the scene in the 1980s, no other female entertainer has come close to Madonna's fame, fortune, and influence. She has had more number-one singles than either the Beatles or Elvis. She's recorded 14 albums and logged five sold-out tours. She's made 16 films and sold more than 100 million records.

Many other female entertainers have looked to men to manage their careers. Madonna, however, has always controlled her own career. It is, perhaps, her business sense that has been her most powerful talent. "She's a great businesswoman," said Seymour Stein, the record company executive who first signed her. "She's very smart and she trusts her instincts, which are great."

"I know that I'm not the best singer and I know I'm not the best dancer," Madonna says. "But I'm not interested in that. I'm interested in pushing people's buttons... ." Madonna has excelled at pushing buttons, and she has become a multimillionaire in the process. She has changed images and personas throughout her career to capitalize on cultural trends.

Madonna is a study in contrasts. She's shocked the world by openly discussing controversial topics. Yet she's also a strict mother, limiting how much television her daughter can watch.

No matter what she does, she seems to cause a stir. "She is what I call a true star," said a musician/ producer close to her. "Even after all these years, I am still curious what she eats for breakfast and that is because she is inherently interesting."

Madonna might add that she's also inherently changing. "People have always had this obsession with me, about my reinvention of myself," she said. "I just feel like I'm shedding layers. I'm slowly revealing who I am."

LITTLE
NONNI

MADONNA LOUISE VERONICA CICCONE
was born August 16, 1958, in Bay City, Michigan.
She was the oldest daughter of six children born to
Silvio "Tony" and Madonna Ciccone. Her parents
called the young girl Little Nonni since she and her
mother shared the same name. Madonna had two
older brothers, Anthony and Martin, a younger
brother, Christopher, and two younger sisters,
Paula and Melanie.

Madonna's father was an engineer with the
Chrysler Corporation. The youngest of six children
in an Italian immigrant family, he was the only
Ciccone child to go to college. Madonna's mother
worked as an X-ray technician at a time when few
mothers worked outside the home.

Madonna recalls her childhood as being strict,
full of rules, and very religious. As a child in the
Detroit suburb of Pontiac, Michigan, Madonna
went to church every morning before school. Her
parents were devout Catholics, and they wanted
their children to be that way, too. "I wouldn't have
turned out the way I am if I didn't have all those
old-fashioned values to rebel against," she said.

This portrait of Madonna was taken in 1980.

Madonna's life changed forever when she was five years old. In December 1963, her mother died following a long, painful battle with breast cancer. Throughout the ordeal, young Madonna felt guilt and confusion. "My mother's death left me with a certain kind of loneliness, an incredible longing for something," she said. "If I hadn't had that emptiness, I wouldn't have been so driven."

To make matters worse, Madonna's family didn't discuss Mrs. Ciccone's death until years

Madonna and her father, Tony Ciccone, on Arsenio Hall's talk show in 1992.

later. Madonna felt she had no one to turn to and no one to talk to. She acted out her loneliness and confusion by trying to get all the attention she could. At school, she swung upside down on the monkey bars in front of the boys. She knew she'd get their attention if they could see her underwear. At home, she even danced on the table to get attention.

With her mother gone, Madonna became even closer to her father. She did everything she could to win his approval. When he announced that each child would get a quarter for every "A" on their report card, Madonna became a straight-A student.

When Madonna was eight, her father remarried. Joan Gustafson had been a housekeeper for the Ciccone family before becoming their new stepmother. But Madonna didn't accept her father's new wife. She felt like she had now lost her father as well as her mother.

Things became worse when her father and stepmother had two more children. Suddenly, Madonna felt just like Cinderella. "I have this stepmother," she said. "And I have all this work to do and I never go out and I don't have pretty dresses." Madonna resolved not to need anyone. She also decided she'd never get close enough to someone to have her heart broken again.

DANCE
FEVER

MADONNA TURNED HER BACK ON LOVE, but she didn't turn her back on attention. She continued her quest to be in the spotlight. She refused to dress like all the other kids in her Catholic school. Even if it was only a different bow in her hair or a brightly colored sweater, she wanted to stand out.

She found another way to stand out through dancing. As a child, Madonna loved to dance. She taught neighbor kids how to dance, too. She began taking formal jazz and tap dance lessons at age 10. That same year, she shocked her family and her school when she did a go-go dance for the school talent show. Her costume was nothing more than a bikini and body paint. It was the first in a lifetime of outrageous performances.

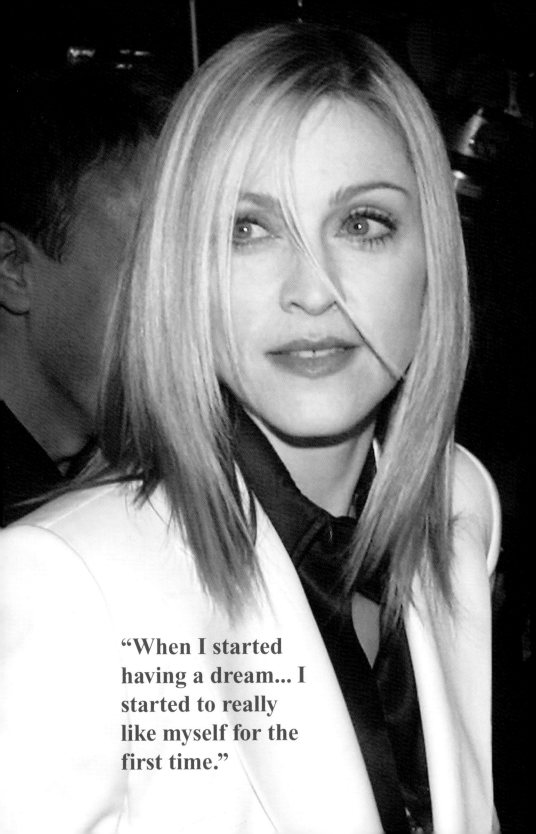

"When I started having a dream... I started to really like myself for the first time."

While in high school, Madonna began to take ballet classes with an instructor named Christopher Flynn, at the Christopher Flynn Ballet School in Detroit. Flynn made her work hard. He also made her grow. "Before I started feeling devoted to dancing, I really didn't like myself very much," she said. "When I started having a dream, working toward that goal, having a sense of discipline, I started to really like myself for the first time."

Flynn also helped Madonna broaden her world beyond home, school, and church. Flynn was a gay man, and he took her with him to local gay disco clubs. Madonna loved the opportunity to dance her heart out. She was soon a crowd favorite at the clubs. Madonna and Flynn became close friends and remained that way until Flynn's death from AIDS in 1990.

When not with Flynn, Madonna had a normal high school experience at Rochester Adams High School. She was a cheerleader and active in many school clubs. She even founded a drama club for students and performed in *Godspell*, *My Fair Lady,* and *Cinderella*. Meanwhile, she maintained her high grades.

Her teachers recall Madonna as a bright, creative young woman with a sparkling personality. It was no surprise when she won a scholarship to the University of Michigan. Flynn had urged her to apply there. She was going to study dance. In the fall of 1976, Madonna left Pontiac for Ann Arbor, Michigan, and the next chapter in her life.

At the university, Madonna took classes in art and music as well as dance. As before, she made a point of standing out from the other students. "I did everything I could to get attention and be the opposite of everyone else," she said. "I'd rip my leotards and wear teeny little safety pins. And I'd run my tights."

As in high school, Madonna continued to frequent local dance and music clubs. She began to date a musician and accompanied him when his band played. Still, it wasn't enough. She was restless. Flynn had encouraged her to try the waters in New York City. After a year and a half of college, she did.

Madonna belts out a song at New York's Radio City Music Hall on June 6, 1985.

A BITE OF THE BIG APPLE

MADONNA ARRIVED IN NEW YORK CITY in July 1978 at age 19. She had $35, and she spent nearly half of it taking a taxi to Times Square. Then she wandered around, feasting her eyes on all New York had to offer. A man spotted her walking around with her suitcase and offered her a place to stay. Not even thinking of her safety, she accepted. Fortunately for Madonna, the man had no bad intentions. He showed her around the city for two weeks and helped her get her feet on the ground.

Shortly after arriving in New York, Madonna applied for a scholarship with the American Dance Festival. She received the scholarship and spent six weeks studying dance at Duke University in North Carolina. Upon returning to New York, she took more classes at the American Dance Center.

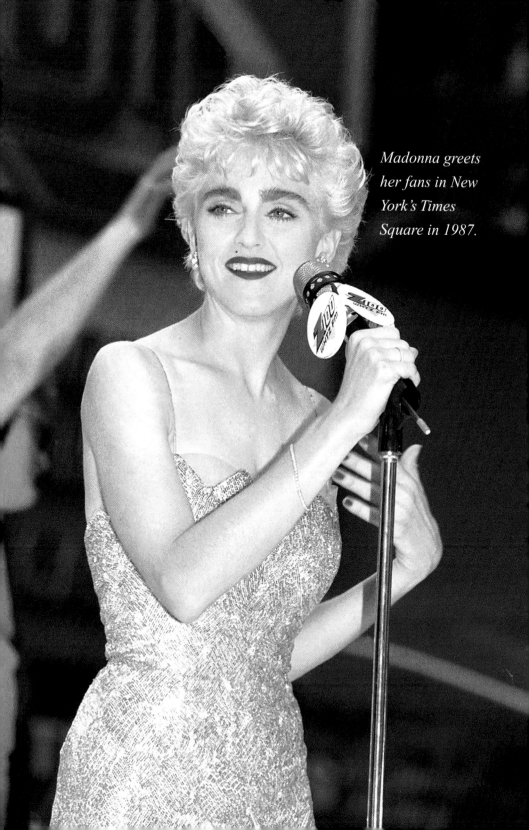

Madonna greets her fans in New York's Times Square in 1987.

Eventually, dancer Pearl Lang picked Madonna to perform with her. Lang recalls that Madonna was a talented, determined dancer. However, she and Madonna often argued. Madonna was by then wondering if her future was as a dancer or not.

While studying at the American Dance Center, Madonna worked odd jobs to earn money. She waited tables, sold doughnuts, and worked as a model for artists and photographers. She lived from hand to mouth. Sometimes she had a shabby apartment to call home. Other times, home was the sofa at a friend's place. Often she did not have money to buy food. Sometimes she charmed men into asking her out on dates so she could get a decent meal.

"All of my boyfriends have turned out to be very helpful to my career, even if that's not the only reason I stayed with them," she once said. Years later, the question of who she was dating would become a hot topic in the press. She dated many men and was usually the one to end the relationships. Madonna biographer Andrew Morton wrote, "Madonna seems to have spent a lifetime searching for love. Yet continually rejecting or discarding those who have loved her, always afraid of being hurt once more."

"Madonna seems to have spent a lifetime searching for love."

In 1978, Madonna met a man named Dan Gilroy. Gilroy was a musician, and he taught Madonna how to play the guitar and the drums.

Madonna gets ready to appear on The Late Show with David Letterman.

Madonna began to think about a career in music instead of dance. She decided to use her talents in dance to break into music.

She auditioned to be a backup dancer for a popular European singer named Patrick Hernandez. She got the job, and in May 1979, she traveled with the act to France and Tunisia. The singer's managers offered to teach Madonna how to sing and become a disco star herself. However, she wasn't drawn to the disco style. She returned to New York and Dan Gilroy.

Soon after her return, Madonna encouraged Gilroy to form a band. They called themselves the Breakfast Club because they often went out for breakfast after rehearsing all night. In the Breakfast Club, Madonna alternated between drums and vocals. Soon, she had a new dream. "People would hear me sing and they'd say, 'Hey, your voice isn't bad.' And I'd say, 'Oh, really?' I mean, I never had any training. I never wanted to be a singer."

Madonna pursued a musical career with her customary passion. She met hundreds of new people, from record store owners to musical talent managers. She practiced playing the drums— sometimes for four hours a day. And she began to write songs.

ROCKIN'
AND
ROLLIN'

WHEN THE BREAKFAST CLUB WOULDN'T let Madonna sing with them as much as she wanted, Madonna left and formed her own band. With her new band, Emmy, Madonna recorded some demo tapes. Then she set out to make sure they were heard.

Madonna had seen to it that she met as many people as possible in the music business. Two of them, Adam Alter and Camille Barbone, became her first managers. In addition to being her manager, Barbone also became Madonna's friend. Sadly, the relationship did not last. Madonna didn't like the direction Barbone wanted to take with her music. She broke her contract with Barbone and Alter in 1982.

Madonna performs on stage during her Drowned World Tour 2001 in Washington, D.C.

In some ways, Madonna didn't need a manager. She had always been skilled at drawing attention to herself. She'd done it when she was 10. Now she did it again. She went from music club to music club in New York City asking the disc jockeys to play her music.

A DJ at the dance club Danceteria noticed how people seemed instantly drawn to Madonna. The DJ, Mark Kamins, had a hunch Madonna had a future in music. He was a talent scout for Island Records. He agreed to use his contacts to help her get a record deal. With Kamins' help, Madonna released her song "Everybody" on Sire Records as a single. It was April 1982, and the song was an instant hit on the club scene. After the release, Madonna went on tour and danced to the music, captivating the crowd and making them enjoy the song that much more.

Madonna now had a contract to produce singles. If the singles were good enough, she would get an entire record. Madonna decided then that she wanted another manager. In fact, she wanted the best one in the business. That was Freddy DeMann. He had been Michael Jackson's manager.

Madonna has
a special magic
that very few
stars have.

As Madonna recalls, she never even gave DeMann a chance to say no to her. "I forced myself into [DeMann's] office and began auditioning there and then—in front of him," she said. "He was quite dumbfounded by my nerve."

DeMann later said Madonna "has that special magic that very few stars have." Eventually, he agreed to work with her. He ended up being her manager for 15 years.

With the Sire Records deal, Madonna also had some money for a change. First, she bought a synthesizer. Then she rented an apartment. And she kept working. Her video for "Everybody" cost just $1,500 to make. Madonna choreographed it herself, and then redid it when one of her back-up dancers failed to show up for the shoot.

In July 1983, Madonna's first album hit the stores. *Madonna* included the singles "Holiday," "Lucky Star," and "Borderline." "Lucky Star" became the first of five straight top-10 hits for the new star. The Beatles were the last musical act to have five consecutive top-10 hits. Madonna was now crossing her own borderline from unknown to star.

DESPERATELY
SEEKING

STARDOM

SALES OF *MADONNA* STARTED SLOWLY. They picked up speed with the release of "Holiday." The song also landed Madonna a spot on the popular TV show *American Bandstand*. *Bandstand* host Dick Clark remembers the first time Madonna appeared on the show. "I watched the kids and they loved her," he said. "She had some sort of bizarre outfit on. She looked different—she was different—and they loved her."

By 1984, *Madonna* was certified platinum and Madonna was a star. She had developed a strong following among young girls who wanted to look and dress just like her. Madonna always has a unique style, and at this point in her career, she mixed and matched thrift shop clothes with tons of bracelets and crucifixes. Young "wannabes" imitated this style. They even tied rags in their hair to copy their favorite singer.

Suddenly, Madonna had a tour full of sold-out shows.

Madonna had made music videos. Now she wanted to branch out to a different kind of acting—movies. She had done roles in the low-budget, never-released *A Certain Sacrifice* and had appeared as herself in *Vision Quest*. Next she landed the title role in the low-budget comedy *Desperately Seeking Susan*. The film did well, mainly because of Madonna's star appeal.

Just before filming *Susan*, Madonna put the finishing touches on her second album. *Like A Virgin* produced the hits "Material Girl," "Angel," and "Dress You Up" as well as the title track. It went platinum within one month. It also put Madonna on the road to her first concert tour. She kicked off the Virgin tour in April 1985, and seats sold out in a flash. Radio City Music Hall, for example, has more than 17,000 seats. When the tickets went on sale, Radio City sold out within 34 minutes.

Suddenly Madonna had a tour full of sold-out shows. However, she'd never done live concerts before. The closest she'd come was lip-synching to her own songs in dance clubs. Many people in the music industry wondered if she would be able to pull it off.

Madonna turned her concerts into theatrical productions. Each song was like a separate music video, with a different look and a different feel. The crowd loved it. In fact, Madonna used many of the same themes from her videos for her concerts.

One of Madonna's most famous music videos is "Material Girl." The video is a tribute to a 1950s performance by actress Marilyn Monroe. Monroe was one of Madonna's idols. In the video, Madonna is dressed much like Monroe. Madonna sings about how she only wants to date rich men.

Many people found "Material Girl" offensive. Madonna said the song was not intended that way. "If they don't get the humor in me or my act, then they don't want to get it," she said.

While filming the video, Madonna noticed a young actor who had come by to watch the shoot. His name was Sean Penn. She talked with him following the video shoot. It was a short meeting, but it made an impression on Penn. He asked Madonna to go out with him and she accepted. The two began a high-profile courtship. It seemed as though whenever they went out, a reporter wrote about it the next day. To make matters worse, Penn hated reporters. He was arrested several times for yelling at and hitting reporters and photographers.

Six months after they began dating, Penn and
Madonna became engaged. They were married on
August 16, 1985. True to her unique style,
Madonna wore a strapless white wedding gown
with a black bowler hat.

*Madonna and Sean Penn
in 1986 at a screening of
Penn's film,* At Close
Range.

SURPRISE FAILURES

SHORTLY AFTER THE WEDDING, THE newlyweds began a joint project. It was a movie titled *Shanghai Surprise*. They began filming in China in January 1986. The movie was riddled with problems from the start. Reporters and photographers continued to hound the couple. Penn lost his temper more than once. Worst of all, the movie didn't turn out as they had planned. In fact, when it was finished Penn and Madonna publicly said it was a bad film.

Madonna quickly redeemed herself with her fans. Before the movie, she had released a third album, called *True Blue*. The following year, she launched her Who's That Girl? world tour. She also starred in a movie by the same name. The movie was another bomb. The tour was a different story.

Madonna performs "Sooner or Later (I Always Get My Man)" from the film Dick Tracy, *during the* 63rd Annual Academy Awards *in Los Angeles. The song won an Oscar for best song.*

**Madonna has always
been very professional
about her career**

Who's That Girl? featured multimedia elements with elaborate staging, costumes, and dancing. Even the name was fitting. Madonna had practically reinvented herself from the time of her first tour. Now the natural brunette had short, blonde hair. She'd also been working with a personal trainer and had developed a more muscular body.

Who's That Girl? was Madonna's most successful effort to date. It also had its share of controversy. One of her songs was about a young, unmarried woman who learns she is pregnant and decides to keep the baby. The song created a stir of controversy from people on all sides of the issue.

Madonna's personal life had its share of turmoil, too. Things with Penn had not been going well. Reporters claimed Madonna's marriage was in trouble. In late 1987, she filed for divorce. The couple tried to work things out but they were unsuccessful. They divorced in 1989.

Madonna had always been very professional about her career. Now, even though her marriage was ending, she was no different. She sought and landed a part in a Broadway play. She agreed to appear in several commercials for Pepsi-Cola. And she began writing songs for her next album.

THE TOP OF HER GAME

IF THE WHO'S THAT GIRL? TOUR HAD BEEN
controversial, it was nothing compared to
Madonna's next album. *Like A Prayer* was released
on March 21, 1989. It showed how Madonna had
grown as an artist. Her early works were light
dance tunes, but her new songs explored complex
issues. *Like A Prayer* explored religion, her
mother's death, and her failed marriage. The
videos she produced were equally complex and
often controversial.

That same year, Madonna heard about the
upcoming film *Dick Tracy*. She very much wanted
a part in the movie. She even agreed to work for
minimum wage to be included. She landed the role
of Breathless Mahoney opposite Warren Beatty's
Dick Tracy. Her character got to perform several
new, and challenging, songs in the movie.

Critics weren't thrilled with *Dick Tracy*. Yet fans enjoyed it. One of the songs Madonna sang in the film won the 1990 Academy Award for best song. She would later release a new album featuring those songs and another hit, "Vogue."

It now had been three years since Madonna had gone on tour. In 1990, she launched her most extensive tour yet. The Blonde Ambition tour visited 27 cities around the world in four months. Blonde Ambition was her most creative and most controversial tour yet. In Italy, Catholic leaders advised people to avoid the concert. They felt Madonna had gone too far in her musical exploration of religious issues.

Fans may have been shocked, but they still flocked to the concerts. Madonna was at the height of her popularity. More than anyone before her, her concerts were blends of music and theater. Madonna was plagued by throat problems throughout the tour, forcing her to cancel some shows.

Madonna had yet another project going during the Blonde Ambition tour. A camera crew followed her around during the tour. They were filming a documentary. It was called *Truth or Dare*. The documentary showed all sides of Madonna. It also showed the hidden side of being a superstar musician. Critics applauded it.

That year alone, Madonna earned $39 million. *Forbes* magazine named her the top-earning female entertainer of the year. There was no doubt by anyone in the industry that the Material Girl had grown up and was at the top of her game.

Fans may have been shocked, but they still flocked to Madonna's concerts.

SINGER
AND
ACTRESS

THE BLONDE AMBITION TOUR HAD BEEN a smashing success. A long-form video from the tour had led to Madonna's first Grammy Award. She'd signed a new contract with Time Warner. And she'd started her own music and film label, Maverick Records.

Now Madonna wanted to focus on her acting career. In 1992, she played a circus performer in the Woody Allen film *Shadows and Fog*. That same year, she was a World War II-era baseball player on an all-girls professional team in *A League of Their Own*. In 1993, Madonna starred as a woman accused of murder in *Body of Evidence*.

But in the early 1990s, Madonna was going through a difficult period. The controversial topics she had addressed in her career had made her unpopular with some people. She received bags of hate mail, and even death threats. Most of her movies had not done well at the box office. And her latest album, *Erotica*, was not selling as well as her previous albums.

Madonna was concerned that her star might be falling. So in 1993, she embarked on another world tour. The Girlie Show tour was even more extravagant than Blonde Ambition. It involved some 1,500 costume changes and 300,000 pounds (136,078 kg) of equipment. The tour was a great success.

Following the Girlie Show tour, Madonna released her album *Bedtime Stories* in 1994. The album included the ballad "Take a Bow." It became her most successful song to date, spending nine weeks at the number one spot on the pop charts. "Take a Bow" showed a new side of Madonna. This one was less controversial, more emotional.

In 1995, Madonna returned to the silver screen. In *Dangerous Game*, she played an actress and abused wife. In 1996, Madonna won the role of Eva Perón in *Evita*. Winning the part was a dream come true for Madonna. *Evita* had been a popular Broadway musical. Madonna had always wanted the title role when the musical made it to film.

Madonna had always felt she would be perfect for the part. Perón had been Argentina's first lady in the 1940s. Like Madonna, Perón had sought the spotlight. She also had been followed by much controversy. Madonna said she related to the character in other ways as well. "It was really

Madonna performs as Eva Perón in the film Evita.

important to her to help and stand up for the rights of people, and I also feel that," Madonna said.

With her performance in *Evita*, Madonna finally received recognition for her acting ability. She won a Golden Globe Award for best actress. While filming *Evita*, Madonna learned she was pregnant. She gave birth to Lourdes Maria Ciccone on October 14, 1996. Madonna's personal trainer, Carlos Leon, was the father of the baby. While Leon continues to be a part of Lourdes's life, he and Madonna never married.

Motherhood and maturity continued to influence Madonna's work and her life. She gave up her three-hour daily workouts and began practicing yoga instead. She became less brassy and more confident. She also studied Kabbalah. Kabbalah is based on a collection of Jewish mystical writings.

Madonna's new spirituality was reflected in her 1998 *Ray of Light* album. The songs were more complex and more spiritual than ever before. They told of her joy at being a mother and her sorrow at losing her own mother. The music included a new style for Madonna called electronica. The album captured three Grammy Awards.

In 2000, Madonna won another Grammy for the song "Beautiful Stranger." It was part of the soundtrack for the movie *Austin Powers: The Spy Who Shagged Me.* She also acted in the movie *The Next Best Thing,* released in 2000. Critics were unkind about her performance, which hurt her deeply. Throughout her career, she has preferred to think of herself as an actress. Yet it is with music that she's had her greatest success.

Madonna poses backstage at the Golden Globe Awards *in Los Angeles in 1997. She won the award for best actress in a musical or comedy for* Evita.

BRITISH
BEAU

IN THE SUMMER OF 1998, MADONNA accepted an invitation to a party near London, England. Her friends, musician Sting and his wife, Trudie Styler, hosted the gathering. At the party, Styler introduced her to a young English film director named Guy Ritchie. Madonna was immediately taken with the handsome young director. "My head didn't just turn, my head spun round on my body," she said later. "I was taken by his confidence."

Madonna and Ritchie eventually began dating. Yet things were difficult. Each had a hectic schedule. They lived on opposite sides of the Atlantic Ocean. Ritchie had recently broken off a long-term relationship. Plus, he was 10 years younger than Madonna. Toward the end of 1999, Madonna made the difficult decision to move to London. "I picked up my life and my daughter and everything and I rented a house in London," Madonna recalled. "That's really when our relationship started to work. But it was a huge sacrifice for me."

Madonna made the best of the move and began recording a new album in London called *Music*. She and Ritchie also had a new project of their own. That project was a baby, due in September.

Madonna developed complications with the pregnancy that summer. Complaining about London hospitals being old-fashioned, she decided to have the baby in Los Angeles. Shortly after moving back, she didn't feel well and asked her staff to take her to the hospital. Once there, doctors realized she was losing blood fast. They performed an emergency cesarean operation and delivered Rocco John Ritchie on August 11, 2000.

Upon returning home from the hospital, Madonna discovered a crumpled paper bag in her bedroom. She was ready to throw it away, but opened it at the last minute. Inside was a diamond engagement ring from Ritchie. Madonna accepted his proposal and began making plans for the wedding.

In typical Madonna fashion, the wedding was just one of many projects on her plate. Not only was the 42-year-old singer recovering from Rocco's birth and running a music empire, but she also was preparing to launch her new album, *Music*. In addition, she gave two invitation-only concerts in November 2000.

Madonna and Ritchie were married on December 22, 2000. The romantic, private ceremony took place at the remote Skibo Castle in northern Scotland. Afterward, Madonna proudly referred to herself as "Mrs. Ritchie."

Madonna with Guy Ritchie, who carries their baby, Rocco, on the steps of Dornoch Cathedral after the baptism of their child on December 21, 2000.

SCREEN DREAMS

IN JUNE 2001, MADONNA KICKED OFF HER Drowned World Tour in Barcelona, Spain. The event quickly became the hottest show of the summer. Ticket scalpers were getting up to $3,000 for one ticket. The 105-minute show was a whirl of music, dance, and light, with extravagant costumes and staging.

A perfectionist, Madonna has always been driven and a hard worker. Each night she lists her goals for the following day. Friends describe her as the first to arrive at work and the last to leave. She expects the same behavior from anyone who works with her.

Madonna is estimated to be worth between $300 and $600 million. She has homes in New York, Los Angeles, and London. Those close to her say she remains a tightwad. She fears that people will take advantage of her because she has so much money. So she watches every penny.

Madonna performs "You Must Love Me" from Evita, *at the* 69th Annual Academy Awards *in Los Angeles, March 24, 1997.*

Madonna performs before more than 10,000 fans in Berlin, Germany, during her Drowned World Tour 2001.

But Madonna can be very generous. She has donated her time and talents to a range of causes, from AIDS to saving the rainforest. Every year on the day after Thanksgiving, she quietly visits children's hospitals. She also gave the proceeds of three Drowned World concerts—nearly $1 million—to help orphans from the September 11 attacks on the World Trade Center and the Pentagon.

One area where she does splurge is artwork. She loves art and has an extensive collection of paintings. She's long dreamed of making a movie about the life of one of her favorite artists, Mexican painter Frida Kahlo.

In the meantime, Madonna continues to evolve as an actress. Her next project is a remake of the 1975 film *Swept Away*. Madonna is planning to play the lead, and her husband will direct the movie.

Madonna has had an exceptional career. The talented superstar is both an award-winning singer and actress. There is no doubt that through her spiritual exploration she will continue to grow in all aspects of her life—as a musician, an actress, a wife, and a mother. Whichever path Madonna chooses next—singing, dancing, or acting—she is sure to be a success.

Madonna holds up her trophy as she accepts the award in the "Best Video From a Film" category for "Beautiful Stranger" at the 1999 MTV Video Music Awards.

Madonna poses with one of her four Grammy Awards backstage at the 41st Annual Grammy Awards *in Los Angeles, February 24, 1999.*

GLOSSARY

AIDS: a condition caused by the HIV virus that weakens the immune system, resulting in deadly infections, some forms of cancer, and a weakening of the nervous system.

electronica: beat-heavy dance music in which the sounds originate from or are altered by electronic instruments.

icon: an image or symbol.

Kabbalah: also called cabala. A spiritual discipline that uses meditation-like practices to commune with God.

multimedia: a combination of media used for entertainment or education, including music, dance, film, slides, and special lighting effects.

platinum: the sale of one million albums.

WEB SITES

Would you like to learn more about Madonna? Please visit **www.abdopub.com** to find up-to-date Web site links about Madonna, her music, and acting career. These links are routinely monitored and updated to provide the most current information available.

INDEX